WHEN THE BEAT WAS BORN

DJ KOOL HERC AND THE CREATION OF HIP HOP

LABAN CARRICK HILL

ILLUSTRATED BY **THEODORE TAYLOR III**

ROARING BROOK PRESS

NEW YORK

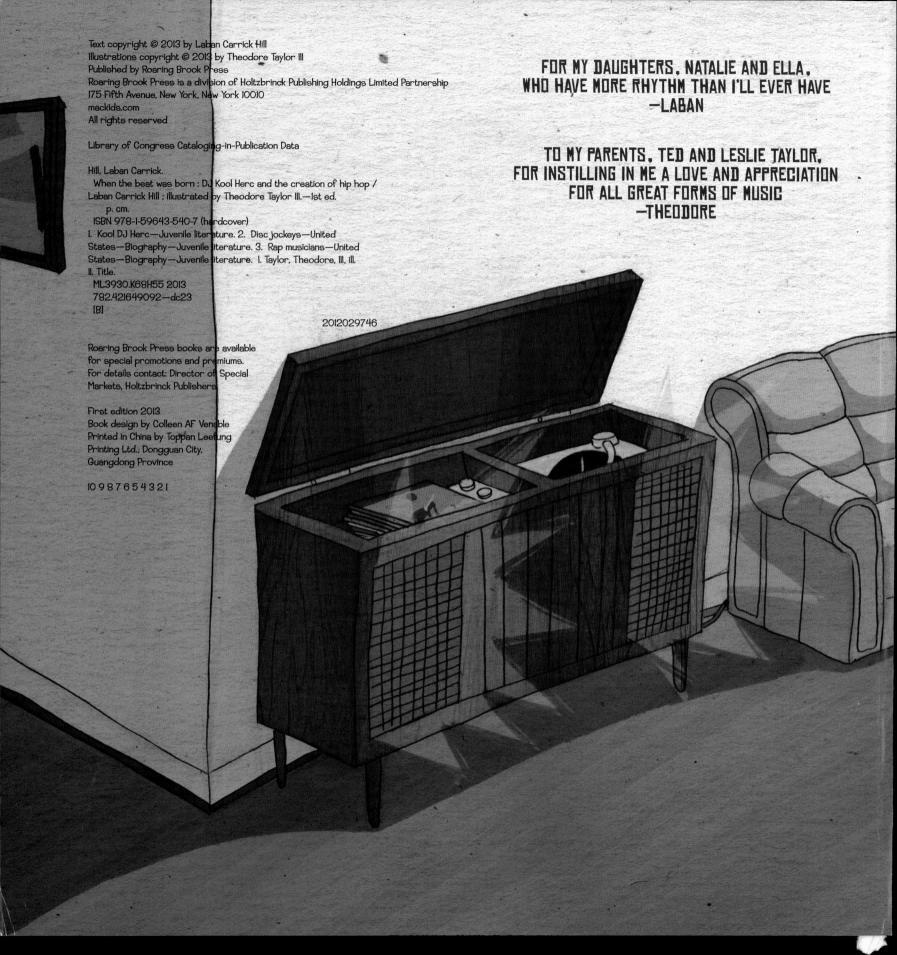

Published by Roaring Brook Press
Roaring Brook Press is a division of Holtzbrinck Publishing Holdings Limited Partnership
175 Fifth Avenue, New York, New York 10010
mackids.com

Library of Congress Cataloging-in-Publication Data

Hill, Laban Carrick.
  When the beat was born : DJ Kool Herc and the creation of hip hop /
Laban Carrick Hill ; illustrated by Theodore Taylor III.—1st ed.
    p. cm.
  ISBN 978-1-59643-540-7 (hardcover)
1. Kool DJ Herc—Juvenile literature. 2. Disc jockeys—United
States—Biography—Juvenile literature. 3. Rap musicians—United
States—Biography—Juvenile literature. I. Taylor, Theodore, III, ill.
II. Title.
  ML3930.K68H55 2013
  782.421649092—dc23
  [B]

                                                    2012029746

Roaring Brook Press books are available
for special promotions and premiums.
For details contact: Director of Special
Markets, Holtzbrinck Publishers.

First edition 2013
Book design by Colleen AF Venable
Printed in China by Toppan Leefung
Printing Ltd., Dongguan City,
Guangdong Province

10 9 8 7 6 5 4 3 2 1

FOR MY DAUGHTERS, NATALIE AND ELLA,
WHO HAVE MORE RHYTHM THAN I'LL EVER HAVE
—LABAN

TO MY PARENTS, TED AND LESLIE TAYLOR,
FOR INSTILLING IN ME A LOVE AND APPRECIATION
FOR ALL GREAT FORMS OF MUSIC
—THEODORE

CLIVE LOVED MUSIC. It didn't matter
what kind. Whether it was a wah wah scat of
a jiving trumpet, a sorrowful twang of sad
voice, or the belting boom of a gospel singer,
little Clive loved the way sound thumped and
bumped all the way down in his stomach. He
loved the way the music made his feet go
HIP HIP HOP, HIPPITY HOP.

Little Clive lived in Kingston, Jamaica. His hero was a DJ named King George who threw the biggest and baddest house parties in the neighborhood of Somerset Lane. On Saturday nights, everybody who was anybody made their way to Somerset Lane for King George's hot dance parties.

Little Clive was too young to go to the parties, so he went to the house when King George and his friends were setting up during the day. They'd arrive pushing a big old handcart stacked with crates of records. Clive had never seen so many records.

He imagined himself as a DJ, surrounded by all those records, choosing just the right song to get the party jamming. He saw himself "toasting" like a DJ- talking and singing over the instrumental B sides of records. Clive dreamed of everyone's feet going HIP HIP HOP, HIPPITY HOP.

Little Clive really wanted to be a DJ.

When little Clive was thirteen, he joined his mama in New York City. Clive wasn't sure he liked his new neighborhood in the Bronx. It was cold. He had to wear a silly winter hat with earflaps, and everybody made fun of him.

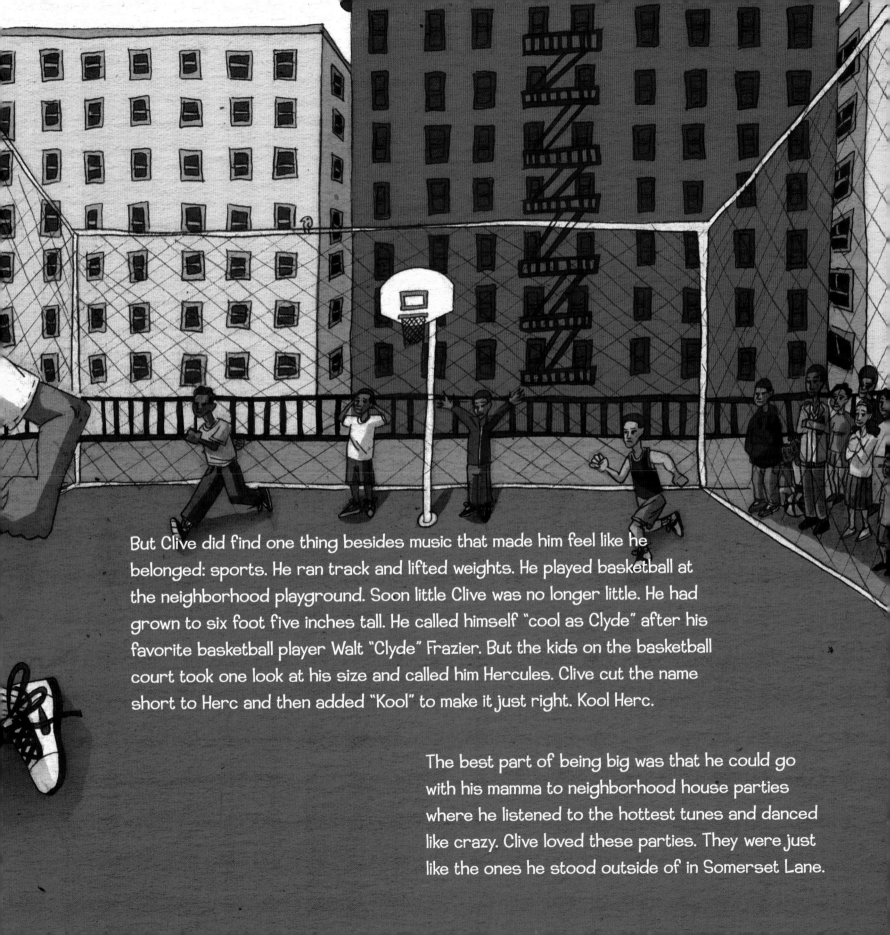

But Clive did find one thing besides music that made him feel like he belonged: sports. He ran track and lifted weights. He played basketball at the neighborhood playground. Soon little Clive was no longer little. He had grown to six foot five inches tall. He called himself "cool as Clyde" after his favorite basketball player Walt "Clyde" Frazier. But the kids on the basketball court took one look at his size and called him Hercules. Clive cut the name short to Herc and then added "Kool" to make it just right. Kool Herc.

The best part of being big was that he could go with his mamma to neighborhood house parties where he listened to the hottest tunes and danced like crazy. Clive loved these parties. They were just like the ones he stood outside of in Somerset Lane.

One day Kool Herc's father bought a monster sound system with giant six-foot speakers. But when he hooked up the system, instead of a really BIG sound coming from the speakers, a little mumbling sound trickled out. Kool Herc spent days switching wires and plugging things into other things, until one day the sound was BIG. Not just big like Kool Herc, but BIG like an entire block in the Bronx.

Kool Herc and his little sister Cindy rented the rec room in their housing project on Sedgwick Avenue. They handwrote invitations telling everybody when and where to get their groove on. They posted cards around the neighborhood. They set up their father's sound system. On the night of the party, everybody who was anybody made their way to Sedgwick Avenue for Kool Herc's hot dance party.

That's when Kool Herc
became DJ Kool Herc.

DJ Kool Herc noticed that dancers danced crazy hard during the breaks in the song when the lyrics ended and the music bumped and thumped. Herc knew that's what dancers wanted so he plugged in two turntables instead of one. He put the same record on both turntables. He set it up so that when one record ended its break, he could flip over to the other turntable and play it again. Doing this over and over, he made a ten-second break last for ten, fifteen, even twenty minutes or more.

Herc remembered the way DJs in Jamaica would chant and toast over the music. He started calling out the names of his friends during the breaks.

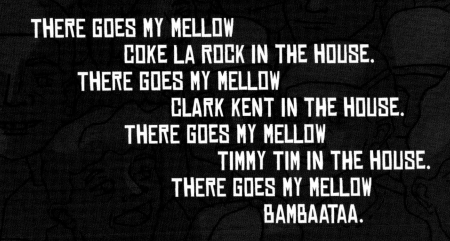

THERE GOES MY MELLOW
COKE LA ROCK IN THE HOUSE.
THERE GOES MY MELLOW
CLARK KENT IN THE HOUSE.
THERE GOES MY MELLOW
TIMMY TIM IN THE HOUSE.
THERE GOES MY MELLOW
BAMBAATAA.

Everybody loved hearing his or her name called out over the music. He'd compliment people on their dance moves. He'd talk about the music and send shout-outs. He'd make up little raps like the jump rope rhymes he heard on the playground. Or he would call, **"HEY, MIKE ON THE LIGHTS, MAKE LIKE A STROBE!"** And Mike would flip the switch on and off.

Over the next year, Herc took his parties to the streets and parks of the Bronx. He plugged his sound system into the lampposts. They pulled so much power that the street lights dimmed–the perfect lighting for a street party.

Kool Herc's music made everybody happy. Even
street gangs wanted to dance, not fight.
Gangs like the Savage Skulls, the Glory Stompers,
the Blue Diamonds, the Black Cats, and the Black
Spades turned into break-dancing crews who
performed some of the slickest moves.

Herc called the coolest dancers break-dancers or b-boys, because they loved to dance the breaks. When Herc would find a really good break, he'd shout, **"B-BOYS GO DOWN!"** Then the break-dancers would cut and jump their gymnastics.

HEY! HEY! CHECK THIS OUT!

THE TOPROCK!

THE DOWNROCK!

Herc gathered a crew of friends to rap behind his DJing. He invited Coke La Rock, a Jamaican friend, to rap. He called him his Master of Ceremonies or MC. Coke knew all about toasting like Jamaican DJs. He was the first of Herc's crew of MCs, called The Herculoids.

Herc would introduce them with a rap:

YA ROCK AND YA DON'T STOP
AND THIS IS THE SOUNDS
OF DJ KOOL HERC
AND THE SOUND SYSTEM
YOU'RE LISTENING TO
IS WHAT WE CALL
THE HERCULOIDS.

Soon kids from all over New York City came to see DJ Kool Herc who threw the biggest and baddest parties on Sedgwick Avenue. Afrika Bambaataa, Grand Master Flash, Jazzy Jeff, and dozens of others all wanted to be DJs just like Kool Herc.

THERE'S NO STORY CAN'T BE TOLD,
THERE'S NO HORSE THAT CAN'T BE RODE,
A NO BULL CAN'T BE STOPPED
AND AIN'T A DISCO WE CAN'T ROCK.
HERC! HERC! WHO'S THE MAN
WITH A MASTER PLAN
FROM THE LAND OF
GRACIE GRACE? HERC! HERC!

Herc didn't just rock the block.
He put the HIP HIP HOP, HIPPITY HOP
into the world's heartbeat.

AUTHOR'S NOTE

In the summer of 1980, I was hired to do market research for a New York City Spanish language television station. My job entailed walking block by block through Harlem and the South Bronx, interviewing bodega owners about the laundry detergent they sold.

In the searing summer heat, I would climb from the depths of the subway and begin my day with a clipboard and a map in hand. Since there wasn't a list of New York City bodegas, I had to just walk until I came upon a store. In the late afternoon, I would approach a corner and hear a loud thumping. The booming would be so deep that it would almost shake the ground. My chest would pound as if it were going to explode. And as I rounded the corner, I would see the most startling sight.

In the media at the time, the Bronx was considered one of most dangerous and desolate places in America. It was America's ghetto. Movies like *Fort Apache, The Bronx*, told stories of the drug-crazed poor committing unspeakable violence on the innocent. Both President Carter and President Reagan toured the South Bronx and gave poverty speeches. But for me, the streets of the South Bronx and Harlem revealed a very different story. In addition to a bustling community of people shopping and living their lives, I discovered a youth movement that was the antithesis of gang violence. When I came around that corner I saw fifty or so

DJ Kool Herc deejays his sister's birthday at 1520 Sedgwick Avenue, Bronx, New York.

Kids start tagging subways and other public spaces with graffiti.

Stevenson High student Kevin Donovan changes his name to Afrika Bambaataa and forms the Zulu Nation.

Herc DJs at the Hevalo Club.

Herc gets Coke La Rock and Clark Kent to rap at parties.

DJ Grand Wizard Theodore accidentally invents "scratching," or nudging a record under the needle, when his mother distracts him by yelling at him.

Hip hop moves beyond the Bronx into New York City's other boroughs.

Rock Steady Crew forms with break-dancers JoJo, Jimmy D, Easy Mike, and P-Body.

Grandmaster Flash forms the influential rap group, The Furious 5.

Sugarhill Gang's "Rapper's Delight" becomes the first rap hit.

Mr. Magic's *Rap Attack* becomes the first hip hop radio show on WHBI New York.

1973 1974 1975 1976 1977 1978 1979

DJ Kool Herc inspires DJs, including Grandmaster Flash and Afrika Bambaataa, to play house and street parties around the Bronx.

DJ/MC Lovebug Starski coins the term "hip hop."

Afrika Bambaataa battles Disco King Mario and sparks DJ battling.

Music industry coins the term "rap music," and shifts its focus from DJs toward MCs.

DJs Grandmaster Caz and Afrika Bambaataa famously battle at the Police Athletic League.

teens dancing some of the most amazing dances I had ever seen. The dances defied gravity and human flexibility. The performances were miraculous feats of physical agility. And they were all done to the beat of records spun by a DJ.

I was so captivated by the music and the dancing that I started going to clubs in the East Village, Tribeca, and the South Bronx where I listened to music like the kids were dancing to in the Bronx and I heard the story of DJ Kool Herc. By 1980, however, it was too late to see DJ Kool Herc perform. The first hip hop record, the Sugar Hill Gang's "Rapper's Delight," had been produced the year before. B-boy dance crews were traveling around the world, from Japan to Montreal, to perform. And in 1980, Afrika Bambaataa and his Zulu Nation began recording, followed by Grandmaster Flash, the Furious Five, and Kurtis Blow.

Thirty years later, this amazing era still defines how I see the world and how I see myself in the world. Back then, no one could have believed that a few desperately poor kids would reinvent American culture. Who could have imagined that a hip hop/jazz infusion group called The Roots would become the house band for *Late Night with Jimmy Fallon*? Who could have imagined that rap would fuse with African High Life into an all-new musical form called Hip Life? Who could have imagined that a rapper would be invited to perform at the White House? Hip hop's rhythms, raps, and its sense of play have not only stuck with me, but have also become the background score for the twenty-first century. So it makes sense now to share the legacy of DJ Kool Herc, the man who first brought the hip hip hop, hippity hop to you. The props are true.

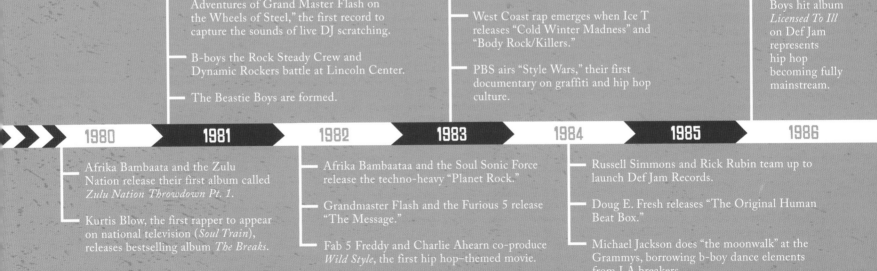

Grandmaster Flash releases "The Adventures of Grand Master Flash on the Wheels of Steel," the first record to capture the sounds of live DJ scratching.

B-boys the Rock Steady Crew and Dynamic Rockers battle at Lincoln Center.

The Beastie Boys are formed.

Run DMC releases "It's Like That," which is a hit on MTV and Top 40 radio.

West Coast rap emerges when Ice T releases "Cold Winter Madness" and "Body Rock/Killers."

PBS airs "Style Wars," their first documentary on graffiti and hip hop culture.

The Beastie Boys hit album *Licensed To Ill* on Def Jam represents hip hop becoming fully mainstream.

1980   1981   1982   1983   1984   1985   1986

Afrika Bambaata and the Zulu Nation release their first album called *Zulu Nation Throwdown Pt. 1.*

Kurtis Blow, the first rapper to appear on national television (*Soul Train*), releases bestselling album *The Breaks.*

Afrika Bambaataa and the Soul Sonic Force release the techno-heavy "Planet Rock."

Grandmaster Flash and the Furious 5 release "The Message."

Fab 5 Freddy and Charlie Ahearn co-produce *Wild Style*, the first hip hop–themed movie.

Russell Simmons and Rick Rubin team up to launch Def Jam Records.

Doug E. Fresh releases "The Original Human Beat Box."

Michael Jackson does "the moonwalk" at the Grammys, borrowing b-boy dance elements from LA breakers.

HIP HOP SELECT BIBLIOGRAPHY

BOOKS

Bogdanov, Vladamir, ed. *All Music Guide to Hip-Hop: The Definitive Guide to Rap & Hip-Hop*. San Francisco, CA: Backbeat Books, 2003.

Bynoe, Yvonne. *Encyclopedia of Rap and Hip Hop Culture*. Westport, CT: Greenwood Press, 2005.

Chang, Jeff. *Can't Stop, Won't Stop: A History of the Hip-Hop Generation*. New York: St. Martin's Press, 2005.

George, Nelson. *Hip Hop America*. New York: Viking, 1998.

Hager, Steven. *Hip Hop: The Illustrated History of Break Dancing, Rap Music, and Graffiti*. New York: St. Martin's Press, 1984.

Kugelberg, Johan, ed. *Born in the Bronx: A Visual Record of the Early Days of Hip Hop*. New York: Rizzoli. 2007.

Forman, Murray and Mark Anthony Neal, eds. *That's the Joint!: The Hip-Hop Studies Reader*. New York: Routledge, 2004.

Nelson, Havelock and Michael Gonzales. *Bring the Noise: A Guide to Rap Music and Hip-Hop Culture*. New York: Soft Skull Press, 2011.

Ogg, Alex with David Upshal. *The Hip Hop Years: A History of Rap*. New York: Fromm International, 2001.

Paniccioli, Ernie. *Who Shot Ya? Three Decades of Hip Hop Photography*. New York: Amistad, 2002.

Shapiro, Peter. *The Rough Guide to Hip Hop*. London: Rough Guides, 2001.

Stavsky, Lois, I. E. Mozeson and Dani Reyes Mozeson. *A 2 Z: The Book of Rap and Hip Hop Slang*. New York: Boulevard Books, 1995.

FILM AND DVD

Beat Street, directed by Stan Lathan. 1984; Santa Monica, CA: MGM Home Entertainment, 2003.

The Freshest Kids, directed by Israel. Chatsworth, CA: Image Entertainment, 2002.

Graffiti Rock and Other Hip Hop Delights, directed by Clark Stanee. 1984; New York, NY: MVD Visuals 2002.

Hip-Hop: Beyond Beats & Rhymes, directed by Byron Hurt. Northampton, MA: Media Education Foundation, 2006.

Scratch, directed by Doug Pray. 2001; New York: Palm Pictures, 2002.

Tupac Shakur: Before I Wake, directed by Sean Long. Santa Monica, CA: Xenon Pictures, 2001.

Wild Style, directed by Charlie Ahean. 1983; Burbank, CA: Rhino Entertainment Co., 2007.

WEBSITES

Columbia College Chicago, rap and hip hop resources: www.colum.edu/cbmr/hiphop/

Hip hop research guide: http://rmc.library.cornell.edu/hiphop/

Hip hop timeline: www.pbs.org/independentlens/hiphop/timeline.htm